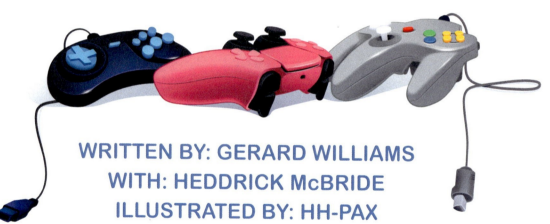

WRITTEN BY: GERARD WILLIAMS
WITH: HEDDRICK McBRIDE
ILLUSTRATED BY: HH-PAX

Copyright © 2024 McBride Collection of Stories

All rights reserved.

ISBN : 9798337973340

SPECIAL THANKS

- **To My Grandmother, Margaret Williams**
  For teaching me how to play video games when I was 4 years old.

- **To My Sister, Tracy Williams-Johnson**
  For always believing in me and seeing greatness in me before I even realized it myself.

- **To Gregory Smiling**
  For always being there to keep me grounded, enabling the growth and maturity I'm living through today.

- **To My Son, Marcus**
  Who inspired the ALEX character in Game Time, and for helping me become an even better person and dad.

- **To R.I.P. Tivon Skinner**
  Who gave me the inspiration to bring a life-changing program to the school system.

- **To Kirk Remekie**
  For opening the door for the PlayMakers to exist within the OSG (Off School Grounds) family.

- **To Ashli Gibbs**
  For being the dot connector to the legend himself, Heddrick McBride, and for bringing us to where we are now with the McBride Stories.

- **To** Jade Johnson
  For inspiring the character Mia. You've become a "Powerful Gamer Girl," with amazing skills. I am so proud of you!

Special thanks to everyone who has rocked with
The Goat of The Game HipHopGamer.
I love you all, and remember, we've got more to do.

"CHARACTER IS YOUR CURRENCY"

CHAPTER 1: PIXEL PIONEERS

Alex and Mia rummaged through their attic, searching for forgotten treasures. Amidst the dust and cobwebs, they stumbled upon a mysterious chest. With eager hands, they opened it, revealing a trove of old gaming consoles and games. "Whoa, check this out!" Alex exclaimed, holding up a dusty cartridge. "It's Super Mario 64! I remember Dad telling us stories about playing this when he was our age."

Mia's eyes widened with excitement as she reached for a faded controller. "And look, it's a Nintendo 64! I've always wanted to try one of these."

The following weekend, Alex and Mia found themselves at a bustling gaming convention. Booths adorned with colorful banners and flashing lights stretched as far as the eye could see, each one offering a glimpse into a different gaming world.

"Wow, this place is incredible!" Mia exclaimed, her eyes darting from one booth to another. "I've never seen so many games in one place!"

"And look at that line," Alex said, pointing to a crowd gathered around a stage.

"They must be unveiling something big!"

As they explored the convention, they met gamers of all ages, each one sharing stories of epic battles and daring adventures. Alex and Mia felt like they had found a new home among fellow gaming enthusiasts.

CHAPTER 2: CHARACTER CREATIONS

    In a dimly lit studio, Alex and Mia sat with a group of game developers, their eyes glued to the screen as lines of code danced across the monitor. "This is where the magic happens," the lead developer said, gesturing to the screen. "Every character starts as an idea, but it's through our work here that they come to life."

    Alex watched in awe as the developer demonstrated how a simple sketch could be transformed into a fully realized character, complete with personality and backstory.

Later that night, Alex and Mia lay in bed, their minds buzzing with excitement. As they drifted off to sleep, they found themselves transported into a world of their own creation.

In this magical realm, they were no longer Alex and Mia but brave warriors embarking on a quest to save the kingdom from an ancient evil. With each step, they encountered new challenges and made new friends, their adventures limited only by their imaginations.

CHAPTER 3: HANDLING WINS AND LOSSES

Back in the real world, Alex and Mia spent countless hours playing games together, their competitive spirits driving them to new heights.

After a particularly intense match, they emerged victorious, high-fiving each other in celebration.

"We make a great team," Mia said, a grin spreading across her face.

"Absolutely," Alex agreed. "We're unstoppable when we work together."

But not every game ended in triumph. There were moments of defeat, of frustration, and of disappointment.

One such moment found Alex on the verge of tears after a crushing loss. Mia sat by his side, offering words of encouragement.

"It's okay, Alex," she said, her voice soft and reassuring. "We'll get them next time. And hey, losing just means we have room to improve, right?"

CHAPTER 4: LINGO LEGENDS

At their next gaming meetup, Alex and Mia found themselves surrounded by a group of seasoned gamers, each one eager to share their knowledge.

"Check it out," one of the gamers said, pointing to a screen filled with colorful icons. "This is where you can customize your character's loadout."

"And this," another gamer chimed in, "is where you can access the game's settings menu."

As they listened and learned, Alex and Mia felt like they were unlocking the secrets of a new language, each term bringing them one step closer to becoming true gaming experts.

CHAPTER 5: VR ADVENTURES

One rainy afternoon, Alex and Mia stumbled upon a virtual reality headset tucked away in a forgotten corner of their room.

Curiosity piqued, they donned the headset and were instantly transported into a world of wonder and excitement. They battled dragons, solved puzzles, and explored ancient ruins, their senses heightened by the immersive experience.

Another day found them dancing and laughing in front of the TV, their bodies moving to the rhythm of the music.

"Nice moves, Alex!" Mia teased, her laughter contagious.

"Thanks," Alex replied.

THE DARKSIDE OF THE SCREEN

While playing their favorite online game, Alex and Mia encountered a group of players who began harassing them with hurtful comments and threats.

Player 1: "Hey, you two are terrible at this game! Why don't you quit and save us all the trouble?"Player 2: "Yeah, go back to playing with dolls, losers!"

Alex: looking upset "Hey, that's not cool. We're just here to have fun like everyone else."

Mia: trying to brush it off "Let's just find another server. These guys aren't worth our time."

Determined to stay safe while gaming online, Alex and Mia attended a workshop on online safety.

Workshop Leader: "Welcome, everyone. Today, we're going to talk about how to protect yourselves from cyberbullying and other online threats."

Alex: "I didn't realize how serious this could be."

Mia: "Yeah, it's scary to think that people can be so mean behind a screen." Workshop Leader: "But there are steps you can take to stay safe. Remember to keep your personal information private, and don't hesitate to report any harassment or abuse you encounter online."

CHAPTER 7: WORLDS OF DIVERSITY

In a game featuring diverse characters from around the world, Alex and Mia felt a sense of connection and belonging.

Alex: "I love how this game celebrates different cultures. It's so cool to see characters who look like us."

Mia: "Definitely! And it's not just about representation. Each character brings something unique to the game."

At a special gaming convention celebrating cultural diversity, Alex and Mia immersed themselves in a world of new experiences.

Booth Attendant: "Welcome to our booth! Would you like to try a demo of our game?"

Alex: "Absolutely! We love exploring games from different cultures." Mia: "And we're always excited to support diverse creators in the gaming industry."

CHAPTER 8: GAMERS FOR GOOD

With the help of their friends, Alex and Mia organized a gaming tournament in their community.

Alex: "Welcome, everyone, to our gaming tournament! We're here to have fun and show off our skills, but let's remember to play fair and respect our fellow gamers."

Mia: "That's right. Good sportsmanship is key, no matter the outcome of the games."

Inspired by their love of gaming, Alex and Mia organized a charity gaming event to raise funds for a local cause.

    Alex: "Thanks to everyone who came out to support our event! With your help, we're making a real difference in our community."

    Mia: "And remember, it's not just about winning or losing. It's about coming together to make a positive impact, both in-game and in real life."

VISIT
www.mcbridestories.com

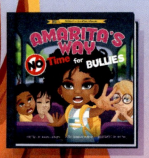
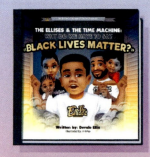

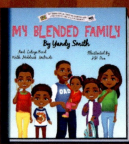

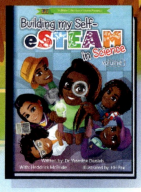
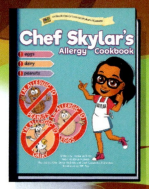

About the Author

Gerard "HipHopGamer" Williams, born and raised in East New York, Brooklyn, began playing video games at the age of 4. His grandmother, Margaret Williams, a hardcore gamer herself, passed down her passion for gaming to Gerard.

Growing up in a challenging environment, gaming became more than just a hobby—it was a lifesaver for Gerard. His grandmother, affectionately known as "HipHopGranny," used video games to teach him life lessons, showing him that, like in games, life is full of challenges, objectives, and tough battles that must be overcome to achieve victory.

In 2008, Gerard was discovered by Torrence Davis, owner of thebitbag.com. This opportunity allowed Gerard to showcase his talents through his weekly "HipHopGamerShow," and learn the art of journalism, paving the way for his professional career in the gaming industry.

After attending E3 in 2008, Gerard never looked back. He mastered the business, built lasting relationships, and revolutionized the industry with his unique energy, style, and skills. Breaking barriers, he opened doors for many Black content creators, giving them a voice and platform.

Today, "HipHopGamer" is recognized as The GOAT of the Game, boasting an unmatched resume. From interviewing the biggest stars in entertainment to being featured as a character and contributing music in AAA video games, Gerard has also made a significant impact on the school system with his Playmakers program and his signature quote, "Character Is Your Currency."

Gerard "HipHopGamer" Williams is truly one of a kind, and his rise continues. In his own words: "1 LOVE & GOD BLESS. In Jesus' name, we pray, AMEN."

Become a Playmaker!

Are you ready to bring an exciting and unique opportunity to your school? Get paid to play games and learn valuable life skills with Gerard "HipHopGamer" Williams! As part of the Playmakers program, students will experience gaming like never before—learning the importance of character, facing challenges, and overcoming obstacles both in games and in life.

Don't miss out on this chance to make a difference in your school community. To bring the Playmakers program to your school, email me at hiphopgamer@hiphopgamer.net. Let's level up together!

Get Paid To Play Games!

Made in the USA
Middletown, DE
29 November 2024